James V: Scotland's Renaissance King

A Tudor Times Insight

By Tudor Times

Published by Tudor Times Ltd

Tudor Times Insights

Tudor Times Insights are books collating articles from our website www.tudortimes.co.uk which is a repository for a wide variety of information about the Tudor and Stewart period 1485 – 1625. There you can find material on People, Places, Daily Life, Military & Warfare, Politics & Economics and Religion. The site has a Book Review section, with author interviews and a book club. It also features comprehensive family trees, and a 'What's On' event list with information about forthcoming activities relevant to the Tudors and Stewarts.

Titles in the Series

Profiles

Katherine Parr: Henry VIII's Sixth Queen

James IV: King of Scots

Lady Margaret Pole: Countess of Salisbury

Thomas Wolsey: Henry VIII's Cardinal

Marie of Guise: Regent of Scotland

Thomas Cromwell: Henry VIII's Chief Minister

Lady Penelope Devereux: Sir Philip Sidney's Muse

James V: Scotland's Renaissance King

Lady Katherine Grey: Tudor Prisoner

Sir William Cecil: Elizabeth I's Chief Minister

Lady Margaret Douglas: Countess of Lennox

Sir James Melville: Scottish Ambassador

Tudors & Stewarts: A collection nof 12 Profiles

People

Who's Who in Wolf Hall

Politics & Economy

Field of Cloth of Gold

Succession: The Tudor Problem

The Pilgrimage of Grace and Exeter Conspiracy

Contents

Introduction 6

Family Tree...7

James V's Life Story...8

Aspects of James V's Life 32

Bibliography 55

James V: Scotland's Renaissance King

Introduction

James V became king aged only eighteen months, and during his minority was at the mercy of the various factions that sought to control the Government – much of the political turmoil being an off-shoot of wider European conflicts. Once he took control of Government himself, James quickly showed that he was made of stern stuff – setting out to tame his nobles and impose his authority, whilst gaining a reputation amongst the ordinary people as a giver of justice.

He was an indefatigable traveller – partly for political purposes, but also to indulge his love of hunting. James also, unusually for a king, spent several months abroad when he visited France to find a bride.

James was not just a soldier, a politician and a judge, all traditional roles of Scottish kings: he was also a musician, a poet and a lover of art and architecture – a true Renaissance Prince.

Part 8 contains James V's Life Story and additional articles about him, looking at different aspects of his life.

Family Tree

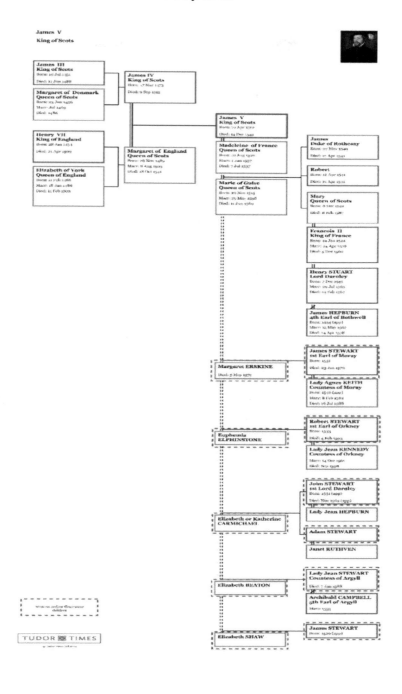

James V's Life Story

Chapter 1: The Early Years (1512 – 1515)

James was his parents' third son, but the first to survive for more than a few months. He was born to the 39-year-old James IV of Scotland, and his wife, Margaret Tudor, at Linlithgow Palace. The marriage of his parents had been intended to reconcile the age-old rivalry between their countries, but unfortunately the *'perpetual peace'* envisaged had not materialised. When James was eighteen-months old, his father marched into England at the head of a huge army, which was shattered at the Battle of Flodden on 9th September 1513 by an army led by Thomas Howard, Earl of Surrey, Lieutenant to Margaret's brother, Henry VIII. James IV and a large proportion of the senior nobles were killed, leaving baby James as king.

The immediate effect of Flodden was to leave Margaret Tudor, under the will of James IV as *'tutrix'* and Governor for James, now King James V, and his tiny heir, Alexander, Duke of Ross, born at the end of the following April. The widowed queen interpreted this role as one of a *'regent'* holding complete power. Margaret was keen to have the position of ultimate authority, as, surrounded by the remaining Scots nobles she felt herself and her young sons to be extremely vulnerable. Her own uncles, Edward V and his brother Richard, Duke of York, had not survived a regency, although they were considerably closer to adulthood than young James V.

Hovering over Margaret and the children were the supporters of John Stewart, second Duke of Albany, who claimed that, as Albany was next prince of the blood, he ought to be appointed Governor in line with the usual Scots custom.

Despite the general misgivings about a Queen who was perceived as pro-English, and strong support for the pro-French Albany, led by James Beaton, Archbishop of Glasgow, Queen Margaret's position was upheld by the Estates (parliament) at Stirling. James was crowned on Wednesday, 21st September 1513 in the Chapel Royal at Stirling Castle, by Archbishop Beaton, to the accompaniment of sacred music, including the Mass for ten voices, *Dum Sacrum Misterium* by Robert Carver, one of Renaissance Scotland's most talented musicians.

Various nobles were appointed to support Margaret, including the Earls of Angus, Huntly, Lennox, Morton and Argyll and a core Council of six was nominated including Lord Hume, Chamberlain; Patrick Paniter, Secretary; Elphinstone, Bishop of Aberdeen, Keeper of the Privy Seal and guardian of the King and Archbishop Beaton, Chancellor. The treasury was found to be empty, but it is apparent from correspondence that 18,000 gold crowns sent by Louis XII to support James IV had been paid over to Margaret by James IV, for safekeeping. In a time when the funding of Government was the King's responsibility, Margaret should have repaid the money to the treasury, but she held onto it, claiming it was to cover her jointure. She effectively stole the money from the Scottish Crown.

In October, Louis XII of France sent his condolences on the loss of James IV. Since Flodden had been a by-product of English-French hostilities, this was the least he could do. Louis told Margaret that he would neither make peace with Henry, nor permit Albany to travel to Scotland without knowing her wishes. In November, the full Scots Council, whilst accepting that Margaret was the legitimate tutrix, sent Islay Herald to France to ask King Louis to send Albany to them for the defence of the realm.   Henry warned Margaret that she should try to prevent Albany returning, and encouraged her in her fears that the Council aimed to take the Governorship from her.

Queen Margaret, having begun well with the rapid organisation of her son's coronation, then placed her position at risk by marrying 24 year old Archibald Douglas, 6th Earl of Angus. Angus was described as a '*young, witless fool*' by his own uncle, Gavin Dunbar, Dean of Moray.

Queen Margaret's match horrified the other nobles and the Scots Estates. It was inconceivable to the sixteenth century mind that a woman could act independently of her husband. For her nobles, it was a truth universally acknowledged that she would be led by Angus, to the detriment of all of the rest of them and they seized on the clause in the will of James IV, stating that remarriage would render his widow ineligible to act as regent. Margaret was determined to hold on to her position and from this time forward, Scotland was plunged into feuding.

Despite having lost her husband to her brother's army, Margaret had all of the English princess's animosity towards France and all of a queen's dynastic eagerness to ensure that her own son should come safely into his kingdom. She turned to Henry to protect her and her sons. In particular, she wanted him to either send an army to protect her and young James, or at the very least, prevent the dispatch of Albany from France. In the aftermath of Flodden, it is hardly surprising that such a course of action led many of the Scots lords to distrust her.

Henry declined to send the army and gave little practical assistance, not even accepting Margaret's proposals for a permanent peace in the troublesome Border region. He did, however, try to persuade Margaret and Angus to take themselves and her sons to England, no doubt with a view to instituting a regency council composed of English sympathisers, and the young king held in England as, effectively, hostage for their good behaviour.

In due course discord amongst the Scottish Lords and between them and Margaret, erupted in a heated dispute over the Archbishopric of St Andrew's. Margaret put forward Angus' uncle, Gavin Douglas. This was opposed by Hepburn, already Prior of St Andrew's. A third candidate for the Archbishopric was Alexander Forman who was the preferred choice of Lord Home.

Gavin Douglas took possession of the Castle of St Andrew's and was besieged by Angus, leaving Queen Margaret and her sons at Stirling. As soon as Angus was out of sight, Lord Home (Lord Chamberlain) and the Earl of Arran raced to Stirling to compel Margaret to attend the Council at Edinburgh where she was forced to give up the Governorship in favour of Albany, having refused a compromise that would have given her guardianship of James, and Albany the political power. Meanwhile, the Earls of Lennox and Glencairn, supporters of Albany, took control of Dumbarton Castle, further lessening respect for the crown.

Albany had been born and brought up in France and Queen Margaret and King Henry continued to put pressure on the new King of France, François I, to hold him back from sailing, but to no avail. François prevaricated for a bit then claimed that as he had already promised the Scots to send Albany over, he could not 'in honour' refuse. Albany therefore arrived at Dumbarton accompanied by eight ships on 18th May 1515 and was installed as Governor of Scotland. His position was formalised by the Estates on 12th July, and Margaret was deprived of her position.

The Council decided that Queen Margaret was no longer to be permitted to keep control of James and his brother as it was material to the effective carrying out of the regency that the King be supervised by the Governor. Nevertheless, she defied the decree and determined to hold onto the boys. She suggested a compromise, whereby the boys would be surrendered to lords chosen by herself, to include her husband, Angus and supporter Lord Home, but Albany refused and besieged Margaret and her sons in Stirling Castle. The Queen eventually surrendered in August, and in one of his first public appearances after his coronation, three year old James symbolically handed over the keys of the castle. On 20th August 1515 James was formally put in the charge of Albany. At the same time, Henry VIII, largely through the efforts of Thomas, Lord Dacre, Warden of the East and Middle Marches, continued to sow dissension by recruiting Scottish supporters through a mixture of bribes, threats, and fomentation of internal disputes – in particular encouraging Lord Home to defect. Home had been offended by some act or remark of Albany's and thereafter could be relied upon to do almost anything to provoke Albany, regardless of the greater good of Scotland. One of his actions was to help Margaret escape for England in September 1515. They were accompanied by Angus and the Earl of Arran. Both Angus and Arran returned and made peace with Albany, but Margaret did not return until 1517.

Chapter 2: Factions and Rebels (1515 – 1528)

James was now, at the age of three, effectively an orphan. For the next thirteen years the various factions ranged at the Scottish court attempted to control his person, and the government. In order to prevent any one group gaining control, it was agreed that various nobles would rotate the guardianship of the king, who was housed in the main defensible castles in Scotland's central belt – usually Edinburgh or Stirling. His most immediate care-giver was Sir David Lindsay of the Mount who was a surrogate father, carrying James in his arms, teaching the little boy to dance and play the lute, and telling him stories. James also had official tutors, the poet, Gavin Dunbar, who remained in post until 1525, John Bellenden, Archdeacon of Moray and William Stewart, a scholar.

James, though he proved to be a shrewd and intelligent man, was not academically inclined. Unlike his Tudor cousins, Mary I, Elizabeth I and Edward VI, he had little skill in languages. He was, however extremely musical (although with a poor singing voice) and able to write poetry in Scots. His chief prowess was in the knightly and athletic accomplishments of the mediaeval king – hunting, jousting, and running at the ring. Once adult, he also showed an appreciation of material beauty and architecture.

By early 1517, Albany was itching to get back to France. He had left his extremely rich wife, Anne, Countess of Auvergne, and his children behind, and he was also eager to take part in what François I hoped would be a continuing series of victories in Italy over Imperial and Spanish forces. Albany nominated a Council to govern in his absence, with Sir Antoine d'Arcy, the *'White Knight'* as his deputy. D'Arcy was well-known in Scotland, having taken part in James IV's tournaments. On arrival in France, Albany was able to negotiate a new treaty in favour of the Franco-Scots Auld Alliance. The Treaty of Rouen of 20th August 1517 committed both countries to mutual aid against any attack by England and also agreed a match for James with a French princess.

Just before Albany's departure, Queen Margaret returned from England, with her daughter by Angus, Lady Margaret Douglas. She was allowed to see James, but he was not permitted to live with her.

Albany's Council of seven soon fell out amongst themselves. D'Arcy was assassinated on 17th September 1517 by the adherents of the Lord Chamberlain, Lord Hume, and replaced as deputy-Governor by the Earl of Arran, next in line to the throne after James and Albany (the little Duke of Ross having died in early 1517). This went down very badly with the Earl of Angus, who, whilst living with another woman, and flagrantly spending Margaret's money, still thought he should be in charge of his step-son's government.

Eventually Angus and Arran came to open blows at the Battle of the Causeway, which was a running battle along the High Street of Edinburgh on 30th April 1520. During the fracas, various members of the Arran party were killed. This fanned the flames of the feud between the Douglases and Hamiltons, Angus' and Arran's kin respectively. Angus' relationship with Margaret had also broken down completely, and she sought a divorce.

In November 1521, Albany returned, and Margaret now gave him her complete support – he had proved a far more respectful and considerate friend than her brother or her husband. Henry VIII moved between alliances with France, which was generally positive for Anglo-Scots relationships, and with the Empire, which was not. Additionally, as the 1520s unrolled, Henry was becoming more concerned about the lack of a male heir. If female inheritance were disallowed (English law did not prohibit it, but it was not a welcome notion), then James V was his uncle's nearest male successor. Henry would always see James in the light of this unwelcome slur on his masculinity.

Angus was banished to France, and rumours spread that Margaret and Albany would marry. Henry VIII add fuel to the flames with an offensive letter to the Estates, claiming that James had been put in the care of a stranger of 'inferior repute' and that Albany's supposed intention to marry Margaret would put James in danger. Margaret was incensed and wrote a stiff reply, pointing out that if Henry continued to be hostile, 'the world will think he aims at his nephew's destruction' – a pointed dig at a man who was Richard III's great-nephew.

The Scots Council, led by Archbishop Beaton, also responded, questioning the possibility of amity between the countries if Henry continued to undermine Albany. Nevertheless, the Scots nobility was not interested in involvement in large-scale military action against England and many of them were very interested in the bribes and promises liberally scattered around by Henry's warden, Dacre. There were large scale border raids led by the Earl of Surrey and Dacre in 1523 in which Jedburgh was attacked and Ferniehurst Castle burnt. Albany was losing his grip on events, and perhaps any will to continue in his role, without more support from the Scots nobles. It was a thankless task, and he left once more for France in 1524, claiming that he had left the country in '*excellent order*' and might return at any time. In fact, he never returned to Scotland although he still took some part in Scottish affairs abroad, particularly in the early 1530s in relation to James' marriage.

Angus now returned to Scotland. From France, he had gone to England where he and his brother, George Douglas, struck up an even closer alliance with Angus' brother-in-law, Henry VIII. For the remainder of James V's reign, Angus and his brother remained in the pay of the English, and promoted English interests, certainly over French interests, and frequently, it would seem, over Scottish interests. It is, of course, possible that they genuinely have believed that a Scotland subjected to English overlordship was a desirable outcome for the country. Henry VIII consistently favoured Angus and his plans over those of Queen Margaret.

Despite their failed marriage, both Margaret and Angus wanted to promote James as old enough to rule without Albany as Governor. The English, too, were in favour, seeing it as an opportunity to keep Albany and the French out. The obstacle to the plan was James Beaton, Archbishop of St Andrew's who remained wedded to the French alliance. Henry, and his chief minister, Cardinal Wolsey, hatched a plot with Lord Dacre to kidnap Beaton, on the pretext of Beaton attending a conference to settle matters on the border. Beaton was too shrewd to fall for it and proposed sending others in his place. As the English had never really intended a peace conference, the idea was abandoned now that the object of capturing Beaton could not be fulfilled. Henry continued with his plans to bribe Scotland into submission, sending money to Arran, and to Margaret and paying for a bodyguard for James.

On 26th July, 1524, James and his mother rode from Stirling to Edinburgh where the nobles swore allegiance to the King, and on 20th August the Estates declared the Governorship of Albany to be ended. James had turned twelve that spring.

Chapter 3: Subjection to Angus (1524 – 1528)

Whilst the nobles, sweetened with English bribes, were prepared to throw off Albany, there was no realistic prospect of James being able to rule unaided. It was ordered by the Estates that Queen Margaret should *'have the rule of her son'* and that he would have four guardians amongst the lords who would take turns to supervise the King, changing quarterly.

Angus was not happy with this, and attempted in November 1524 to seize control of him, but was repelled from an assault on Edinburgh Castle. James and Margaret then established themselves at Stirling, and Angus and Beaton made some sort of private deal. Nevertheless, the rotation of the King's guardianship continued, and included a turn for Angus.

Slightly more cordial relations were established with England during 1524, and in December, Henry VIII wrote to Pope Clement VII, asking him to confirm James' (or rather, Margaret's) nomination for a bishopric. Henry also wrote to James, thanking him for his *'good understanding'* of Henry's letters, *'as proceeding from the fresh wit and great towardness of wisdom which is reported to be in him (James)'.*

He went on to assure James that one of his own principal concerns was James' safety and honour. All the blame for the troubles of the past eleven years were obviously the result of Albany's machinations and henceforward Henry and James could live in perfect peace (provided James followed his uncle's advice, of course).

During 1525, France suffered a major defeat at the hands of the Emperor Charles at the Battle of Pavia, so had little time or inclination to get further involved in Scots affairs. With a weakened ally, and many of the Scots Lords in English pay, the Estates agreed a three-year truce with England in July of 1525, which was eventually ratified in June 1526. The Estates of 1525 consisted of some ten earls, nine senior lords, five lesser lords, eight commissioners for burghs and twenty clergy.

In June 1526, the lord in charge of James, according to the scheme of rotation, was Angus. On 14th June, James was declared to be of full age. According to Scots law, James could now cancel any grants made during his minority, however, Angus had no intention of letting him wield authority. His plan was to control James, whilst negating any arguments that the King should move to another guardian once Angus' term ran out. James was furious, but unable to escape from Angus' clutches.

His anger towards the whole Douglas clan grew during this period, and, as Angus was strongly representing Henry VIII's interests, the seeds of suspicion between uncle and nephew were sown. A new Privy Council, largely made up of Angus' supporters was appointed, with himself as Chancellor.

In 1526, Queen Margaret wrote to Henry VIII, saying that James, despite being recognised as of age by the Estates was in 'thraldom' to Angus, and had been forced by Angus to write various letters to Henry and the Pope criticising Archbishop Beaton.

James, desperate to escape from Angus, made an agreement with the Earl of Lennox, and a scheme was hatched to rescue the King when he rode with Angus to the Borders, to attempt to punish the notorious reivers, the Armstrongs. Lennox' ally, Scott of Branxholme, mounted an ambush (known as the Battle of Melrose) to rescue James, but Angus had the support of Lord Home's men, and retained control.

James did not give up, and a further armed confrontation took place at Linlithgow, when Lennox again brought soldiers, but was defeated by Angus, now allied with Arran.   During this confrontation, George Douglas told James that they would hang onto his person, even it if meant him being torn in pieces. Lennox was killed, Arran cried crocodile tears, and then withdrew from Angus' party. Angus was reconciled to Beaton (at the price of a large bribe) but his brother suspected Beaton's motives. Angus, according to Henry VIII's envoy was *gentle and hardy, but wants wit.*

In January 1528, James, presumably forced by Angus, wrote to Cardinal Wolsey in England, asking him to request Henry VIII to prevent the return of the Duke of Albany, although the likelihood of Albany wanting to return was small.

Chapter 4: James Takes Power (1528 – 1534)

At Easter 1528, now aged sixteen, James called his Privy Councillors together and confronted Angus, claiming that he was promoting his own relatives at the King's expense; failing to keep peace in the Borders (thus undermining the three year truce with England) and offending foreign ambassadors. Angus promised to mend his ways, sending a force to the Border to hang a few outlaws, and summoning troops.

In May James wrote to Henry VIII that these troops, far from being levied to protect the Borders, were part of a plot by Angus to kill him

(James). Somehow, between 27ᵗʰ May and 30ᵗʰ, James gave Angus the slip, and appeared at Stirling, where his mother was in residence. James was now supported by Arran, Beaton (who, as anticipated by George Douglas, had double-crossed Angus), Lord Maxwell and the Earl of Argyll. In his triumph, he wrote to his uncle, Henry VIII, proclaiming that Angus and his brother had been commanded to give themselves up, but had disobeyed and were wreaking havoc in the country.

The Estates were summoned for 2ⁿᵈ September, and Angus should have attended, but failed to do so. He claimed that his disobedience in not giving himself up was justified as he and his supporters would have been in danger of their lives. As for the troops that had been gathered in May, it was done by the King's own command to take reprisals against the Border warlords.

Angus retired to his castles, first Coldingham, then Tantallon, which he fortified (but *not to the prejudice of the King*). He still hoped to negotiate from a position of strength. James besieged Tantallon, but his artillery was captured by Angus (who returned it so as not to offend too deeply).

The three-year truce with England had expired, and Henry and James' commissioners met to agree new terms. The English initially sought the reinstatement of Angus, but the Scottish commissioners refused, and queried why Henry would want to support a rebel. It also became apparent to Henry and Wolsey that Angus had nothing like the support in Scotland that he had previously claimed.

The English, now aiming to ally with France against the Emperor (partly in the hope of French support for Henry's annulment, which was largely occupying his mind) chose not to press the point of Angus' reinstatement and peace was renewed. This did not stop the English from continuing to subsidise Angus' in '*doing all the mischief he could*' in subsequent years.

A five year peace was concluded in December 1528, and Angus and his daughter, Lady Margaret Douglas, who had been held by her father as a bargaining chip against her mother, Queen Margaret, were exiled to England. This did not prevent him working to undermine James from the safety of England.

James took up his authority with panache, rewarding and promoting men who had supported him, or been close to him such as Gavin Dunbar, who was now appointed as Chancellor. One of James' early actions was to set about improving matters on the Border, where he led an expedition in 1529 with the aim of punishing criminals. Unfortunately, it met with little success.

He also wrote to Henry VIII, thanking for his support during his minority (presumably his tongue was firmly in his cheek) and then explaining his own activities in trying to keep the peace. He mentions that the Earl of Northumberland has been rather slack about attending the regular meeting days, and was not redressing the crimes of English subjects in Scotland.

The following year (1530), suspecting some of the nobles with interests in the Border of undermining his authority, he arrested a number of them, including the Earl of Bothwell, and Lords Home and Maxwell. He then gathered a larger force and captured a large number of miscreants, some of whom gave surety for good behaviour, but some were executed. Although James has subsequently been criticised for severity, the men executed were blackmailers (in the sixteenth century sense of extorting protection money), thieves and burners of women and children in their homes.

James also faced trouble in the Highlands and the Isles. The Isles had only been integrated with the Scottish Crown in the reign of his father,

James IV, and there was continued strife between the different clans, and between them and the central authority.

Under Albany, Argyll had effectively been given lieutenancy over the southern Isle, and the Earl of Huntly over the northern lands. Both protested their loyalty and eagerness to pacify the clans for the benefit of the King, but clan feuds and revenge seem to have been part of the plan. In 1530, Argyll, who had been a supporter of James against Angus, sought permission to proceed against Alexander of Islay. After some hesitation, this was granted, but Argyll died shortly after.

With the help of James' illegitimate half-brother, the Earl of Moray, and the new Earl of Argyll, the clan chiefs submitted, but complained about Argyll's actions. James investigated, and stripped Argyll of his offices, granting them to Alexander of Islay. One of the underlying causes of this renewed trouble in the Highlands and Islands, was MacLean of Dowart's ill-treatment of his wife, Argyll's sister. He is said to have chained her to a rock, and left her to drown. She was rescued by a passing boat, and her brother, in revenge, broke into MacLean's bedchamber when he was in Edinburgh in 1523, and stabbed him to death.

Flexing his muscles, James wrote a very short letter to Henry VIII, saying that he could not grant Henry's continuing requests for the restoration of Angus to office, without 'great inconvenience' and asking him to desist from intervening in the matter.

The exertion of control by James was not popular with his lords either in the Borders or the Highlands, and there was an attempt led by Bothwell, Argyll, Maxwell, Moray and others to overthrow him. James managed to suppress this, by dint of reconciliation with Moray. He then set about giving Henry VIII a taste of his own medicine by paying for Highlanders to assist Irish rebels against England.

Border raids continued, with James and Henry writing to each other, blaming the other's officers for not keeping the peace and giving redress as required. In 1532, eager to improve relations with France, in support of his annulment, Henry was more conciliating to James, suggesting that he attend the planned meeting at Calais, between Henry and François, and inviting James to travel there via England. He also sent expensive gifts. James declined to visit on this occasion.

Eventually, a further truce was agreed in May 1534, to last a year longer than the death of either monarch. Again this was part of a wider peace between France, England and Scotland. James received the Order of the Garter from England, and the Order of St Michel from France in token of everyone playing happy families.

Following James' election to the Order of the Garter, Henry sent Lord William Howard (brother of the Duke of Norfolk) and Garter King of Arms to take James the accoutrements of the Order, including the Garter Book. The book itself was an elaborate and expensive confection. Written on vellum, with illuminated letters and arms, it was bound and gilded, covered in purple velvet, and laced with purple silk laces. Attached by green and white silk laces were the seals, and the bag was enclosed in a bag of red satin, lined with red sarcenet and drawn with red silk laces. The bag was ornamented with Venetian gold, and encased in a box.

Chapter 5: Love and Matrimony

James IV had been a notorious womaniser, but James V looked fair to outdo his father in this respect. He had children by at least five different women during the decade from 1528. These relationships are remembered because they were with women of the nobility – he probably had numerous other mistresses as well. James took responsibility for his children and, unlike in England, there seems to have been little stigma attached to illegitimacy, although it debarred them from the Crown.

The most important of the ladies in James' life was Margaret, daughter of the 5th Lord Erskine. Margaret bore him a son in 1531, James Stewart, later Earl of Moray, Regent of Scotland. Another mistress was Elizabeth Beaton (or Bethune), great-niece of the Archbishop. Elizabeth's daughter, Jean Stewart, became Countess of Argyll and a close friend of her half-sister, Mary, Queen of Scots.

A marriage had been mooted between James and his cousin Mary, daughter of Henry VIII and Katharine of Aragon, as early as 1524. This would, to an extent, have solved Henry's succession problem, if they had married young and produced a son. But there were obstacles – first, Henry wanted a son of his own; second, the English were adamant that they did not want a Scottish King; and third, after the annulment proceedings began, which would render Mary illegitimate, James declined to take an interest in tarnished goods.

James also considered marrying Margaret Erskine, but to do that she would need to have her marriage to Sir Robert Douglas of Lochleven, which had taken place in 1527, annulled. James made the request of Pope Clement VII, but it was refused, and James was either less enamoured of Margaret than Henry was of Anne Boleyn, or more genuinely religious. He accepted the Pope's ruling.

Other candidates for the post of Queen of Scots were Catherine de Medici (niece by marriage of the Duke of Albany). Catherine was also a niece of the Pope, and as Duchess of Urbino in her own right, was a promising bride. She was soon snapped up by François I for his own son (the thought of Catherine de Medici as Queen of Scots is fascinating....). There was also Mary of Austria, the widow of the King of Hungary, and Regent of the Netherlands for her brother, Emperor Charles. Other possible brides were Christina of Denmark, the Emperor's niece, and Isabelle, sister of the King of Navarre.

The Treaty of Rouen of 1517 had envisaged a French princess as a bride, and James now decided that this was still the right answer. King François' eldest living daughter, Madeleine, suffered (probably) from tuberculosis, and François was reluctant for her to marry. Instead, in 1534, he offered Marie of Bourbon, daughter of Charles, Duke of Vendome. Marie was a '*princesse du sang*', that is, a lineal descendant of Louis IX and thus worthy to be a queen. Albany was in favour of the match, and set his secretary, Nicholas Calvinet, to work with James' Secretary, Thomas Erskine of Brechin, to agree terms.

James demurred – he wanted a daughter of François. He informed François that anything else would be a departure from the Treaty of Rouen, and require the consent of the Estates. François offered the same dowry as he would give with his own daughter which partially satisfied James, who then sent an envoy to meet Marie and report on her looks and deportment. If the envoy considered her suitable he could confirm her dowry with François, and arrange for her dispatch to Scotland, before winter.

Eventually, agreement was reached on 29th March 1536. James however, rather than waiting for Marie to be delivered to him, resolved to visit France in person. He instituted a Regency Council consisting of Archbishops Beaton and Dunbar, the Earls of Eglinton, Montrose and Huntly and Lord Maxwell. He set sail from Leith but was driven back to shore and took refuge in Whithorn, Galloway, before embarking again from Kirkcaldy on 1st September, 1536, with numerous earls in attendance and a huge retinue. The King's flagship was the *Mary Willoughby*.

On arrival in France, he went first to Marie of Bourbon's home, at St Quentin, but, for unknown reasons, broke off the match. Later chroniclers say that Marie was disabled in some way, based on a comment of Marguerite d'Angouleme, sister of François, that Marie was 'sore made awry', but, presumably, if that were the case, James would already have known. Marie's death in 1538 was attributed by the chronicler Leslie to her distress at being jilted by James.

When he left St Quentin, James headed south to meet François, and insisted that he would only marry Madeleine. Perhaps he fell in love with the sixteen year old girl, or perhaps he wanted the prestige of being the King of France's son-in-law. It appears, however, that Madeleine was just as keen as James, saying she wanted to be a Queen before she died. François, although certain that the Scottish climate would be his daughter's death-knell, eventually agreed. The marriage treaty, signed at Blois, renounced any claim by Madeleine or her children to the Crown of France. Her jointure was to include the earldoms of Ross, Strathearn, Orkney and Fife as well as several palaces and lordships. The dowry and wedding gifts her father gave were munificent.

James and François appear to have got on well, and James certainly enjoyed his stay in France to the utmost.

On 1st January 1537, he and Madeleine were married at Notre Dame. They left France in May 1537, travelling up the channel, with an escort of ten French vessels. Sailing up the English coast, they purchased fresh fish and meat from Bamburgh and other towns along the Northumbrian coast.

Madeleine was richly provided with jewels, furs, silver plate, furniture and hangings, to make her new home comfortable. She also had a long train of attendants, including her former governess and doctors as well as her furrier, butcher and secretary.

Sadly, despite all the cosseting that James and her father could give her, Madeleine died on 7th July, 1537, having been Queen of Scots for just six months. She was buried at Holyrood Abbey.

James mourned her sincerely, but personal grief could not interfere with government diplomacy, and in June 1538 he married a second time, to Marie of Guise, niece of the Duke of Lorraine, and widow of Louis d'Orleans, Duke of Longueville.

Chapter 6: James as King

Throughout his reign, James made sustained and widespread efforts to improve justice and the rule of law throughout his kingdom. One of his acts was the founding of what is now the Court of Session of the highest civil court in Scotland. He also commissioned the Register House within Edinburgh Castle, for the housing of national archives at a cost of £120 Scots.

James was keen to portray Scotland as an important kingdom in its own right. He spent lavishly on renovating and improving the palaces of Stirling and Falkland in particular, creating Renaissance fantasies similar to those to be found in the Loire valley. One of his greatest expenditures was on his series of tapestries, now recreated at Stirling Castle.

He also played a complex diplomatic game. With England in the grip of religious turmoil, James took the opportunity to increase his standing with European powers and isolate England. In particular, he took care to increase his position with the Emperor Charles, at one time hoping for a marriage with a relative of his. James also kept a cordial relationship with his own cousin, Christian of Denmark.

In one of the least attractive actions of his reign, James took revenge on the sister of Angus. Lady Janet Douglas, Lady Glamis, was accused in

September 1528 of having poisoned her husband, John Lyon, 6th Lord Glamis. The charge was dropped, and Janet was given a licence to go on pilgrimage. But in December of the same year, she was accused of having abetted Angus in holding the King against his will. This charge, too was dropped, and she married again.

James, however, had a long memory, and in July of 1537, Janet was again arrested, charged this time with conspiring to poison the King, of witchcraft and also with corresponding with her exiled brothers, the Earl of Angus and George Douglas. English commentators (who may well have been biased) said there was little evidence against her, but nevertheless, she was burnt to death – the standard punishment for a woman accused of treason or witchcraft.

In May 1540, James and Marie had a son, another James. With the succession hopefully now assured, King James set out on a journey round his kingdom. In a fleet of twelve ships, he set sail in June, accompanied by the Earls of Huntly and Argyll, as well as Cardinal David Beaton, who had followed his uncle, James Beaton, as Archbishop of St Andrew's on the elder Beaton's death in 1539.

The progress stopped at numerous places along the Scottish coast, the court would then disembark and camp near the sea-front, before embarking on hunting and hob-nobbing with the local gentry as well as holding Justices in Ayre. The purpose of the progress was three-fold – for James to show himself to his people at all levels of society; to show his power to any nobles who thought they were far enough away from the King to disobey him; and to see justice done, one of James' priorities.

He was back in the south in time for Marie to conceive and bear another son in April 1541. In a tragedy for the couple that is hard to imagine, both little boys died on the same day – 28th April, 1541 (some accounts say within a couple of days of each other). The Dowager Queen,

Margaret, wrote to Henry VIII at the end of May about the distress of both parents. Queen Margaret herself was ailing, and died in October of that year, at her castle of Methven. James ignored her request (she had not made a will) that her jewellery be given to his half-sister, Lady Margaret Douglas, now a leading light of Henry's court, and kept it himself.

During 1541, the idea of a meeting between James and Henry VIII was mooted. Such a meeting had frequently been talked of, and both sides had made soothing noises about its desirability, but no concrete arrangements had ever been made, although there had been detailed discussions in 1536.

Henry decided to make a progress to the north of England, to exert his authority and overawe with his presence following the Pilgrimage of Grace. It was suggested that James should travel to meet Henry at York, where Henry arrived, accompanied by his fifth wife, Katheryn Howard, on 16th September 1541. The English royal party waited for some ten days, but James did not appear. With no legitimate children, and a not-unfounded fear of kidnap, James, who had carefully never actually committed himself, declined to make the journey.

Henry was outraged at the insult, which was yet another nail in the coffin of Anglo-Scots relationships. With the death of Queen Margaret the following month, there was no-one who could even try to make peace between uncle and nephew.

During 1540, James had promulgated new ordinances for the army. Every man between sixteen and sixty was liable to be called out for defence, and had to be ready to muster at the named point within 24 hours of the call, armed and arrayed in a jack or brigandine (a protective corselet that covers the upper body, padded and with small metal plates sewn in to deflect arrows), together with gloves and a gorget (neck protector).

Scots armies were traditionally made up of 'schiltrons', that is, phalanxes of foot-soldiers in tight formation bearing extremely long spears or pikes. The weapons the ordinary men were to bring could include any of: spear, pike of six ells in length, culverins, hand bows and arrows, cross bows, halberds, axes or two-handed swords. Only earls or lords could be mounted, and any horses brought by lesser men were to be used for carriage.

With the final breakdown of amity between James and Henry, it seemed that military action might be necessary.

In June 1542, Thomas Howard, 3rd Duke of Norfolk, accompanied by Sir Robert Bowes, invaded Scotland at the head of an army of 8,000 men, including Douglas supporters. The Earl of Huntly, and Lord Home met the invaders near Kelrose, and scored a decisive victory at the Battle of Haddon Rig. Bowes, who had had charge of a party sent to harass Jedburgh, was taken prisoner, but soon released.

Following this, James sent further dispatches to England, in July and August to make peace. His overtures were not accepted, and the Duke of Norfolk mustered an army of some 20,000 that crossed the border at Berwick and set about the usual burning and pillaging around Kelso and Roxburgh.

James called his levies to meet at the Borough Muir, just as his father had done in 1513. His army numbered somewhere up to 30,000 – it is difficult to be more accurate as contemporary sources tend to exaggerate numbers. He set out towards Fala Muir (where the Battle of Pinkie would be fought some five years later), but was greeted by the news that Norfolk and his men had retreated homeward. At this point, James wanted to carry the war into the enemy camp, but his nobles refused to support him. They did not want war with England.

James was obliged to disband the majority of the troops, but retained about 18,000, who were sent to attack in the west. James himself rode with the army, but mindful of the dire consequences of his father's death in battle, did not plan to take part himself, instead remaining at Lochmaben, about twenty miles inside the Scottish Border. He had also complained of illness in a letter to Queen Marie, which may have been another factor in him not joining the army.

The Scots crossed the border and advanced southward to cross the River Esk near Longtown. The English were surprised, having expected Haddon Rig to be followed up by a crossing on the east, but the Warden, Sir Thomas Wharton, an extremely experienced commander, rustled up a defensive body of about 3,000 and proceeded north from Carlisle.

With the numbers the Scots had, it seemed that victory was a foregone conclusion, but matters went awry. There was quarrelling and dissension amongst the Scots leaders. Lord Maxwell and Sir Oliver Sinclair both claimed to be in command. The Scots plan had been less one of a battle, and more a retaliatory raid, and, when Wharton approached on 24th November, 1542, the Scots were not in battle array but were busy about cattle-rustling and burning of farmsteads. The Scots were trapped between the rivers Esk and Lyne.

After intense fighting, the Scots broke and attempted to flee across the Solway Moss. The English captured the Scots artillery and the royal standard – a terrible humiliation. Whilst casualties in the fighting were small, many Scots were drowned in the Moss, and some 1,200 were taken prisoner, including the Earls of Cassilis and Glencairn and Lords Maxwell and Fleming.

Nevertheless, this defeat need not have been a worse outcome from Scotland than many of the other Border skirmishes. James, although humiliated by the loss of his royal standard, and many of his nobles, could have rallied and continued with his reign – England did not have the resources to occupy and subdue Scotland for the long term. James, however, was not just sick, he was dying.

He rode from Lochmaben to Linlithgow, where Queen Marie was awaiting the birth of their third child, then on to his favourite palace at Falkland. He heard the news of his daughter's birth on 8th December, but died on the night of the 14th – 15th or possibly 15th – 16th of December. Chroniclers liked to say he died of a broken heart, following the misery of defeat at Solway Moss, but the truth is more prosaic – he died of that perennial curse of soldiers, dysentery, or possibly cholera.

The last words ascribed to him (although they are probably apocryphal) are 'It cam' wi a lass, and it'll gang wi' a lass', reference to the Stewarts' inheritance of the throne through Marjorie, daughter of Robert the Bruce. He was aged thirty. James was buried at the Abbey of Holyrood, together with Queen Madeleine and his sons by Marie of Guise.

*

James had been an effective king for the fourteen years of his personal rule. He was not as personally popular with his nobles as James IV had been, seeming to have more of the suspicious temperament (not without reason!) of his grandfather, James III. Had he not died so prematurely, it is likely that he and Queen Marie would have had more sons, and the fate of the British Isles might have been quite different.

Aspects of James V's Life

Chapter 7: Religion and Reform

James V was castigated by English Protestant writers of the nineteenth century as *'priest-ridden'* and superstitious. Even later writers cite the prominence of ecclesiastics such as Cardinal Beaton as proving that James was a benighted bigot. However, this interpretation is so heavily influenced by the partisans of the Knox and the Scottish Reformation that it hardly reflects the truth of politics and religion in Europe in the first half of the sixteenth century.

Whilst James IV had been a promoter of learning, a supporter of Erasmus and a well-informed and educated man himself, the vast majority of the upper classes in Scotland were still of the mediaeval mind-set that left learning to clerics, and lawyers. There was neither the wealth, nor the stability in society that could support the level of patronage of education that was beginning to be seen in England, through patrons such as Lady Margaret Beaufort and Bishop Fox. James V's education had been truncated, and, although he was an intelligent man, there is no sign of him having an academic bent.

With no highly educated men outside the Church, and, to a lesser degree, the law, it was natural that James, in common with every mediaeval and early modern king, should have clerics as his chief advisors. The appearance of the layman Thomas Cromwell as Henry VIII's most prominent minister was almost unprecedented.

As the Church was almost the only career open to an intelligent man of good family, who was not the oldest son, the higher ranks of the clergy were filled with men who may have had little or no real religious conviction, beyond unthinking conformity to traditional beliefs and practices. It was also a convenient way of securing lands and income for illegitimate sons, particularly for kings, who arranged benefices for them when they were well below the canonical age.

James IV's illegitimate son, Alexander, who was tutored by Erasmus, was an archdeacon at nine years old, and Archbishop of St Andrew's (the primacy) at a mere eleven. James V's own brood of sons benefited similarly with at least six of them being preferred to office whilst children, including the priories of St Andrew's, Whithorn and Charterhouse.

In Scotland, as elsewhere, the senior ecclesiastical offices gave access to lands and relatively high incomes. Although the Pope was the ultimate decision maker, since he did not usually have any day to day knowledge of the offices in question (apart from the Bishoprics) he tended to accommodate requests from the King, or other ecclesiastics or nobles whom he wished to favour (or, sadly, but truly) those who paid the largest bribe. Whilst an office was vacant, or if the holder were a minor, the income would slip into the King's pocket.

Earlier Scottish Kings had negotiated an eight month period for them to nominate a new Bishop; James pursued his rights in the matter of benefices vigorously, and frequently wrote to Rome complaining if his wishes were not respected.

After the Battle of Flodden, when the Pope had been strongly in favour of the English position, Henry VIII petitioned Pope Leo X to rescind the Scots King's right to recommend bishops and to insist that Henry be consulted over the filling of the many bishoprics left vacant after the battle. Unsurprisingly, the Scots were infuriated by this interference. The quarrel came to a head over the filling of the

Archbishopric of St Andrew's (vacant as Alexander Stewart had fallen at Flodden).

The story is complex, but worth telling, as it is a microcosm of how the whole ecclesiastical system was run.

There were five contenders in the race.

Queen Margaret, supported by Henry VIII, nominated Gavin Douglas, uncle of her new husband, the Earl of Angus. Douglas immediately occupied the Archbishop's castle. The Pope had his own candidate, his nephew, Cardinal Innocenzo Cibo. Albany (who had not yet been appointed Governor, and was still in France) was in favour of Andrew Forman, Bishop of Moray, Bishop of Bourges and Commendator of several abbeys. The fourth nomination, by the Council, was Bishop Elphinstone of Aberdeen. Fifthly, there was John Hepburn, who was already Prior and Dean of St Andrews and had begun collecting the income.

The Pope, Leo X, sent an envoy to take possession for Cibo but he was refused entry to the country by the Council, who then wrote, in King James' name, protesting against this encroachment on the Crown's privilege of nomination. The Pope reconfirmed James' rights, and dropped Cibo, doing a deal with Forman who agreed to resign his bishopric of Bourges in Cibo's favour. Forman was then appointed by Leo.

Hepburn besieged Douglas and drove him out of the castle. The Council wrote to the Pope, claiming that Forman was a rebel and should not be granted the Archbishopric. When Forman arrived in Scotland, he was prevented by the Council from leaving his Priory at Whithorn, but, after Albany's installation as Governor, the Council was persuaded to accept him as Archbishop (Elphinstone considerately having died in the interim) and in the following year, he also became Papal Legate. Hepburn and Douglas compromised their differences by an exchange of cash, and the grant of one of the minor offices of Douglas to a Hepburn relative, whilst Douglas received the Bishopric of Dunkeld.

This unedifying spectacle was typical of Church governance and undermined respect for the Church. As elsewhere in Europe, the senior clergy also flagrantly broke their vows of celibacy, many having long term relationships and children, disgusting on-lookers with their blatant hypocrisy.

Queen Margaret's secretary described the situation:

'Every man taks up abbacyis that mayest: thay tary not quhilk (until) benefices be vacant: thai tak tham or (before) thai fall...'

In 1517, when Luther took up his pen to complain of the conduct of the Church hierarchy, his arguments fell on fertile ground all over Europe, and Scotland was no exception.

The first mention of Luther is in the Parliament of 1525, which James presided over, although he was still under the control of Angus. Parliament passed *'An Act Anent (concerning) Heresy'* which proclaimed that importing and/or reading his works, on pain of forfeiture. The majority of the works – Luther's writings, and perhaps early translations of the Bible – were likely to have come into Scotland through its eastern ports, where trade with Germany and the Low Countries was frequent. This prohibition was repeated and amplified in the Parliament of 1535. Merchants bringing such books in were to have their ships confiscated.

James' own education had been in the hands of Gavin Dunbar, who became Archbishop of Glasgow in 1524, and, exceptionally, was permitted by the Pope to operate outside obedience to the Primate, the Archbishop of St Andrew's (by this time James Beaton, Forman having died in 1521). James obviously trusted Dunbar, who was granted the office of Chancellor as soon as James could act for himself. Relations between Dunbar and Beaton were poor and even worse with James Beaton's successor as Archbishop, Cardinal David Beaton, who was translated there in 1539.

Dunbar was a cleric of the old school – pluralist, militant and a politician rather than a man of religion. However, he was happy to use his spiritual power to political effect. In 1525, in pursuit of the truce with England, he issued a curse on the Border Reivers, which is wonderful to hear. This *'monition'* which was to be read by every parish priest to his congregation is pages long, but a couple of choice sentences illustrate:

'I curse thair heid and all the haris of thair heid; I curse thair face, thair ene [eyes], thair mouth, thair neise, thair toung, thair teith, thair crag [neck], thair schulderis, thair breist, thair hert, thair stomok, thair bak, thair wame [womb], thair armes, thair leggis, thair handis, thair feit, and everilk part of thair body, frae the top of thair heid to the soill of thair feit, befoir and behind, within and without..... I curse them within the house, I curse thaim without the house, I curse thair wiffis, thair barnis [children], and thair servandis participand with thaim in thair deides. .. thair cornys, thair catales, thair woll, thair scheip, thair horse, thair swyne, thair geise [geese], thair hennys, and all thair quyk gude [livestock].'

There was the issue of money, as well. One of the defining grievances against the Catholic Church all over Europe was the wealth of its upper ranks and, often, the monasteries, whilst parish priests were frequently poor and ill-educated. The doctrine of purgatory and payment for Masses for the dead, weighed heavily, and the payment of the best cloth and a cow for funeral masses impoverished many.

With traditional churchmen such as Beaton and Dunbar in charge, there was little chance of any interest in Church reform, particularly where it questioned Church authority, and in 1528, the first Protestant martyr in Scotland, Patrick Hamilton, Abbot of Ferne was burnt.

Hamilton had had plenty of warning that he was to be arrested, and Beaton had intimated that his escape was desirable but he had not left Scotland by the time men arrived to arrest him. Hamilton was well connected – nephew to Arran, Albany and Lennox, and second cousin to the King, but this did not save him from a mismanaged burning that lasted six hours because wet fuel was used. His example of fortitude did, however, sway many to listen to the message of reform.

In 1539, a further five men were burned in James' presence. Burning was the punishment prescribed by law for heresy in Scotland and across Europe – if a heretic refused to recant, the secular authorities had no choice but to carry out the sentence. In other instances, such as that of David Stratilon in 1534, it appears that James exhorted the accused to recant.

For James, there was a political element to his faith, as well as a religious one.

In the early 1530s when his uncle, Henry VIII, was renouncing Papal authority, he made overtures to James to join him. Henry and his ministers became increasingly concerned about the risk of invasion by France or the Empire to uphold traditional religion, and it would have been a great comfort to him to know that Scotland, the back door to England, would join him. He suggested James join with him in rejecting the 'pretended' authority of the Bishop of Rome, who sought to keep princes in ignorance. James responded that he would:

'hold by God and Holy Kirk as our ancestors have done these thirteen hundred years.'

A later suggestion to James that the monasteries ought to be put down to enable him to take their property was met with the answer that he could not see any benefit in so doing:

'[they have stood] these many years, and God's service maintained and kept in the same, and I might have anything I require of them...'

For James, the advantage lay all on the side of conformity. The more unpopular Henry was with the Pope, and the European monarchs, the more they would caress him. In 1532, James instituted the College of Justice, the forerunner of the Court of Session. To do this, he needed money, and Clement VII agreed to the taxation of clergy – which seems only fair as Church lands in Scotland were worth about ten times the value of Crown land. James was thus able to access Church wealth without going to the extremes of Henry VIII's dissolution programme.

James was further honoured by the Pope (Paul III) in 1537, who dispatched a cap of maintenance and sword to the King, as he travelled through France. James tipped the Papal messenger 400 crowns and gave him a horse trapped in velvet.

James could not, of course, be unaware of the need for change, and happily listened to satire upon the ignorance, superstition and venality of the average priest, composed by his childhood mentor, Sir David Lindsay of the Mount.

But there was a difference between condemning poor practice and rejecting the authority of the Church or its doctrines. The Parliament of 1541 clearly set out the official position of James and the three Estates, with legislation that comprised the following for management of the Church (paraphrased – see Acts of Parliament of Scotland):

1. The Holy Sacraments were to be honoured, as in time past
2. The Virgin Mary was to be worshipped and reverenced and prayed to intercede with the Holy Trinity for the welfare of the King and Queen and for peace and concord amongst Christian people. The saints were also to be honoured and invoked.
3. There was to be no questioning of the Pope's authority, on pain of death and confiscation

4. Reforming kirks and kirkmen – a long list of exhortations for clerics to set a good example and look after their parishes and parishioners in accordance with church teaching

5. There were to be no private conventions to dispute scripture

6. Abjured heretics may not discuss religion, abjured or suspected heretics may not hold office

7. There is to be a reward for those that reveal conventions for disputing scripture or heretics

8. No-one is to damage or dishonour statues of the saints

9. It will be treason for anyone to try to install a bishop or abbot, other than as nominated by the King of the Pope.

In other orders, James forbad the Church to exact death duties.

With a King and clergy committed to holding to the old faith, it seems unlikely that the Reformation would have gained much ground in Scotland, had James lived, especially if he had kept up pressure for internal reform. His early death, however, opened the door to a much more radical change in religion, with the appearance of George Wishart and John Knox.

Chapter 8: The Gudeman of Ballengeich

A story is often told that James V would dress up (or rather, dress down) as a yeoman farmer, and would walk amongst his subjects incognito, calling himself the Gudeman of Ballengeich (ie the tenant farmer of Ballengeich, a place near Stirling). Thus disguised, James would find out about life from the perspective of his subjects, rather than just hearing what his nobles or clergy told him. Whether the facts are true or not, the story points to a belief that James was interested in the life and fate of the common man, and this certainly seems borne out in his attitude to one of his chief roles, that of giver of justice.

In England, the role of judge had long been delegated from the King to professional judges, but in Scotland, it remained an important part of his kingship.

He would travel to the '*caput*' or main town in the various sheriffdoms (from which the word shire derives) and hear the most serious case at sessions called Justices in Ayr. These would last from four to seven days, with Sundays always excluded. The day to day matters of justice were dealt with in the Barons' courts, with the baron, or laird, having '*right of pit and gallows*' and jurisdiction over '*life and limb*'.

The justice system in Scotland was complex, but important features include the fact that prison as a punishment did not, for the main part, exist. The pannel (accused) would be held in the sheriff's gaol, but only until the trial. If he were filed (convicted) his punishment would be either a physical one – hanging, the stocks etc, or being outlawed for a sum of money – what we would term a fine.

In addition, criminal justice was not just a matter between the Crown and the wrong-doer, but was also a matter for the victim. The criminal would need to compensate the victim (or his family) through assythment, for which he would have to find sureties until it were paid. Once assythment had been agreed, the malefactor would be outlawed for a sum and the King would grant a pardon, conditional on that being paid. There were variations around this, if the victim could not be satisfied, or there were no sureties. In some cases, the King could grant a pardon without the victim being satisfied, but this was rare.

The Justices in Ayre were not generally courts for the finding of guilt, instead, pannels who had agreed assythment were brought forward for pardon, and to be brought back into the king's mercy. An important part of the system was the use of sureties. These were the kinsmen and the laird of the pannel, who would also come into the court and, collectively, assume responsibility.

There seem to have been few crimes for which assythment, and subsequent pardon was not possible, even murder. One such was 'common' theft, which was a general accusation of theft but without a specific victim identified, so no assythment could be made. Common thieves were frequently hanged. This was the charge usually brought against the border reivers.

One of the most well-known cases of James dispensing justice, rather than granting pardon following assythment, was that of Johnny Armstrong. Armstrong and his clan were notorious reivers – raiding across the border, stealing cattle, raping, murdering and burning. In 1530, when James set about trying to reduce the levels of crime in the area, he promised Armstrong safe-conduct, but then broke his word and hanged Armstrong and thirty-six of his clan.

He also personally heard the case of William Cockburn of Henderland, panneled and fined for inbringing (abducting) an Englishman and his son. Cockburn was beheaded and his goods forfeit to the Crown.

At the same Justice in Ayre, on 18th May 1530, Adam Scot of Tuchelaw was found guilty of taking black-mail (protection money) from poor tenants, and was similarly beheaded.

A major problem with the justice system was identified as the frequent 'non-compearance' (non-appearance) of the pannels, meaning that justice was protracted and that the injured could gain no relief. A statute of 17th June 1535 was enacted to deal with that, by proclaiming that a second non-attendance would result in confiscation of goods and the accused being 'put to (the) horn' – that is, the town crier would wind his horn three times, then publicly declare him a rebel. Additional provisions were made for restitution of costs where one party falsely accused another, and unusually, gave a punishment of imprisonment of a year and a day, for failure to pay the costs.

Later acts required the bailiffs and stewards of the court to attend in person to ensure justice was properly done and that cases were to be heard within fifteen days.

When James first became king, there was no separate court for civil cases – everything was disposed in the Baron's court, or at the Justice in Ayre.

In 1531, Clement VII issued a Papal Bull, granting James the right to tax Church property to fund a new civil court.

On 17th May 1532, legislation was brought into Parliament for the setting up of a

'college of cunning and wise men, both of the spiritual and temporal estate, for the doing and administration of justice in all civil actions'

The court was set up with 14 judges, half laymen, half clerics, and was to sit for three terms in each year. Justice was to be administered equally to anyone before the court. There was provision for the Lord Chancellor to preside, were he available.

Additional rules were set out for how defendants were to be summonsed, for removing notaries who were not competent, and for ensuring that notaries were properly introduced to the courts. Losers of lawsuits were to pay the other party's expenses, as modified by the sheriff. Documents brought in evidence had to be signed as well as sealed, or witnessed if the person could not write.

The college was the forerunner of the present Scottish Court of Session, the highest civil court, and preserved in the Act of Union of 1707 *'for all time coming.'* James could be justly proud of his creation.

Chapter 9: French Fashions

In February of 1536 a marriage was agreed between James and Marie of Bourbon, daughter of the Duke of Vendome, a relative of King François I of France. The original intention of the Treaty of Rouen of 1517, had been for James to marry a daughter of the King, but his two elder daughters had died young, and the next in age, Princess Madeleine, who was not quite sixteen, was in frail health, probably suffering from tuberculosis. François therefore proposed Marie of Bourbon, offering her with a dowry as great as that of a Princess of France.

James, after initially protesting, and seeking a bride amongst the flock of female relatives of the Emperor, whether genuinely, or to concentrate François' mind, agreed to the match. He gave authority to the Duke of Albany to conclude negotiations and send the bride to Scotland. For some reason, however, he changed his mind about waiting at home for his bride, and decided to go to France to fetch her himself.

He requested a safe-conduct to travel through England, but this was refused. The Duke of Norfolk wrote to Henry VIII and the Council, saying that, although he was surprised that James had not asked Henry directly, he did not think there could be a problem with James' request, other than in the matter of expense.

Henry replied, that no King of Scotland could be entertained in England except as a vassal, for 'there never King of Scots into England in peaceful manner otherwise'. In addition, since James had failed to meet Henry as previously mooted, citing that he feared betrayal, Henry could not allow him or his wife to travel through England, because if there were any mishaps, Henry would be suspected.

Following this ungracious response, James was obliged to sail all the way. In July, he set out, but was driven back by storms. After regrouping, on 1st September 1536 he sailed again from Kirkcaldy, in Fife (or possibly Leith), with seven ships, landing at Dieppe on 11th of the month. He took no chances with leaving potential troublemakers at home, and was accompanied, amongst others, by the Earls of Argyll, Rothes and Arran and the Lords Fleming (his brother-in-law) and Maxwell.

There is some inconsistency as to whether James went first to Paris, or to the Duke of Vendome's chateau (variously reported as at St Quentin in Picardy, but more likely the Vendome chateau near Tours), but little doubt as to what happened in either place.

Lindsay of Pittscottie claims that he went to the chateau in disguise, but that Marie recognised him from a painting she had been given, and picked him out. Her perspicacity may have owed something to the fact that he would be obviously foreign, spoke poor French and was red-headed.

For some undisclosed reason, having met Marie and spent eight days at her father's home, near Chartres, being feasted and honoured, and practically smothered in cloth-of-gold, James no longer wished to go through with the match (it is unlikely she would have been allowed to refuse). Marie of Bourbon died the following year – according to Pitscottie, she pined away following the heartbreak and dishonour of being jilted.

When James arrived in Paris the French court was not in residence so James amused himself, apparently 'incognito', much to the disgust of Sir George Douglas, brother of James' enemy, the Earl of Angus, and currently in Paris in English pay. According to Douglas, James, who had 'beggared Scotland' to take £19,000 Scots to cut a magnificent figure in France, ran up and down the streets of Paris, with no more than a couple of servants, buying everything in sight, fondly believing himself unrecognised, whilst the shopkeepers pointed and whispered '*Voila le roy d'Ecosse*'. Perhaps it was a matter of etiquette, that, until he had waited upon the King himself, he should not admit to being in the country.

In his running up and down the streets, James did some serious shopping. He purchased a great diamond, fifty-five spears, some for tournaments, others for battle, tipping the spear-makers lavishly, and four white feathers at a cost of 12 francs for his bonnet (as a comparison, the diamond cost him 8,787 francs).

In due course James travelled to La Chapelle, near Lyons, where the King and court were in residence, in deep mourning following the death of François' eldest son. Some reports have Madeleine as present, although too ill to ride, others state that she and James did not meet until the court was at Amboise. With the appearance of his royal guest, François was roused to activity. James made a good impression, and there are reports of the two Kings hunting together at the Chateau of Loches, in the Loire.

Perhaps the loss of his son (his third child to die) made François reluctant to disappoint his daughter, who, despite her illness, apparently wanted to be a Queen. More romantically, she and James may have become genuinely attached – although there was an eight year age gap. It is certainly likely that James was attached to the French alliance in principle, and the 100,000 livres tournois dowry plus an annual pension that was on offer. Despite his misgivings about sending her to the damp climate of Scotland, François agreed to the marriage, and they were betrothed on 26th November 1536.

The court returned to Paris, and on 31st December made a state entry. James made a splendid figure, dressed in crammasy (red or crimson) velvet, lined with red satin with raised gold work and 116 22-carat gold buttons, with lapis-lazuli. According to his wardrobe inventory, he had another fifty similarly elegant and extravagant outfits. Complaint was made by the burgesses of the French Parliament that they had been obliged to dress in their red coats and process in front of anyone other than a King of France, but François replied that he wished James to be treated with as much honour as himself.

On 1st January 1537, James was led in procession by François to the cathedral of Notre Dame, where he married Princess Madeleine. Once married James continued shopping, buying quantities of textiles and tapestries. He also received twenty fine horses from François, all trapped with enamelled harness. François gave Madeleine the run of his cloth stores, allowing her to take as much cloth-of-gold, velvet and satin for her clothes and those of her ladies-in-waiting as she liked. The young Queen also received quantities of jewels from her father.

Whilst in Paris, James bought two huge beds, furnished with green velvet and damask curtains and counterpanes. The fabrics had come from Genoa and Florence, and, in total there were some seventy yards of fabric used. The craftsman who made the bed hangings, one Guillaume Petit, was paid twenty crowns to up sticks with his wife and children and move to Scotland.

The young couple left for Scotland in mid-May (after a delay owing to Madeleine's illness) and arrived on 19th May 1537.

Once home, James was determined to recreate what he had seen in France, on both the inside and outside of his palaces. He had been accompanied to France by a French mason, Moses Martin, who was already in his employ. Martin was named as master-mason not long after arrival in France. This suggests that James was planning before he left home to find out more about the latest styles in architecture.

François' spending on the chateaux of the Loire was no doubt famous in every court in Europe.

Queen Madeleine, and later, James' second wife, Marie of Guise, both received Falkland Palace and Stirling Castle as parts of their jointure and both properties received extensive make-overs, partially funded by the lavish dowries that both ladies received. (Marie's was only two-thirds of Madeleine's, but still a princely sum.) More beautiful beds were furnished, and the King expanded his collection of tapestries.

Stirling Castle today has been renovated to show how the royal apartments looked in the 1540s, after James' death, but still occupied by his widow, and heavily influenced by French Renaissance taste.

Chapter 10: Following the Footsteps of James V

The numbers in the article below correspond to those on the map which follows.

On Saturday, 10th April, 1512, James V was born in Linlithgow Palace (1), which had been his father, James IV's, 'morning gift' to his bride, Margaret Tudor. The palace, which is now an evocative ruin, was one of the most modern and comfortable in Scotland. He was baptised the following day, which was Easter. Despite his parents' marriage having been intended to promote peace between England and Scotland, within eighteen months the countries were at war, and James IV was killed at the Battle of Flodden. Young James was now King, aged seventeen months.

Margaret took him to Stirling (2), one of the most defensible castles in all of Scotland, situated at the crossing point on the Forth that had seen numerous battles, including Bannockburn, two hundred years before, and Sauchieburn in 1488. James was crowned in the Chapel Royal at Stirling on 21st September.

During James' minority, there were constant quarrels over guardianship of his person, and he was usually moved between Stirling, Edinburgh Castle (3), and Holyrood Palace (6). In September 1517, an outbreak of plague in Edinburgh led to him being moved to Craigmillar Castle (4), about three miles south-east of the city centre. He also spent time at Dalkeith Castle.

In 1524, James was declared of an age no longer to need a Regent or Governor. Instead, he was to be under the guardianship of his mother, and various lords who would take turns to supervise him. Matters did not go as expected, and Archbibald Douglas, 6th Earl of Angus, and estranged husband of Queen Margaret, took control of James.

For the next four years, Angus ruled James and the Government, setting himself up as Chancellor, and giving key offices to his friends and family. James chafed under his government, but despite a couple of attempts was unable to break away until May 1528. Accounts vary as to whether James was at Edinburgh or Falkland Palace (5) when he managed to escape to Stirling in May.

Now sixteen, James began his personal rule. One of his early actions was to march on Tantallon Castle (7), Angus' stronghold on the northern coast of Lothian and besiege it. The King arrived with impressive artillery but despite battering away for nearly three weeks could not mount an effective attack. He was unable to capture the castle or Angus (who was elsewhere) and lifted the siege. In May 1529, Angus, still being hunted by James, managed to slip away to England. Tantallon was taken into royal hands.

Over the next few years, James travelled extensively around the south of Scotland, largely in the cause of putting an end to the constant lawlessness in the Borders. During two expeditions of 1529 and 1530, he visited Haddington, Jedburgh, Peebles, Lindores, Crammald (now Cramalt Tower) and Magetland (the area around today's reservoir of Megget Water).

He also ventured further north, to Allan Water, Perth, Dundee and Dunkeld. He did not generally stay anywhere for more than a few days, and most trips were from his main residences at Stirling, Edinburgh (both the Castle and the Palace at Holyrood) or Linlithgow and then back.

One of James' chief interests, as for so many noblemen of the time, was hunting. There are frequent references in the Lord Treasurer's accounts for the expenditure on dogs, horses and hunting equipment, as well as for hunting trips, particularly near the delightful Falkland Palace, the hunting lodge that he spent significant sums of money upgrading.

In the summer of 1533, he went further afield on a hunting trip, to Blair Atholl Castle (10), seat of the Earl of Atholl. The whole court went on the jaunt, James, Dowager Queen Margaret, the Papal envoy who was visiting and the King's councillors. During the visit, some 600 animals were slain – deer of various kinds, wolf, foxes and even wild cats. The Earl had built a splendid wooden palace for the King, which, on departure, was burnt. James told the astonished Papal Envoy that it was the custom for countrymen to burn the place they had slept in the night before!

After leaving Blair Atholl, James went on to Dunkeld and Perth, before travelling west to Glenorchy and Inverary (9).

On 1st September 1536, James set sail from Kirkcaldy to visit France, where he spent some nine months, returning in May of the following year with his bride, Madeleine of France. Madeleine took up residence at Holyrood Palace, but died within two months of her arrival, and was buried in the Abbey. The mourning for the young Queen was intense, and orders had to be given for black cloth to be brought in from Dundee to Edinburgh for mourning clothes, the city having run out of black. A further order was given, preventing any increase in the price of black cloth.

The following June, a new wife and queen arrived, Marie of Guise, at Balcomie Castle (8) in Fife. James and Marie were married at St Andrew's, where they then spent six weeks before moving to Cupar, to Falkland for hunting and then on to Stirling and Linlithgow.

On 1st March 1539, James was at Edinburgh, where he witnessed the burning of five 'heretics', before returning next day to his Queen at Linlithgow. Whilst James and Marie do not seem to have been particularly attached to each other, they spent plenty of time together, hunting, visiting the shrine of St Andrew's and enjoying their building projects. According to one source, they went on a pilgrimage in their ship, the Unicorn, to a shrine on the Isle of Man (12), but it seems unlikely. At some point (the dates are unclear) they also travelled to Aberdeen (13), and spent some two weeks there.

Whilst at Falkland Palace, it is likely that James would have visited his menagerie. These were popular symbols of Renaissance power, and James was the happy possessor of various wild animals, including a lion. The creature had been bought in Flanders, where James' man was outbid by his uncle's, but Henry VIII then sent it as a gift.

During the summer of 1540, James went on an extended tour, by sea, around Scotland. He was not accompanied by his Queen, possibly because she had only just had a baby, or perhaps he saw the mission as essentially a demonstration of power in areas of Scotland that were not fully controlled by the Crown, and hence potentially dangerous.

He sailed with some twelve ships as far as the Orkneys (which had come to Scotland as surety for the dowry of his grandmother, Margaret of

Denmark, and never been redeemed), and then through the Hebrides and the Western Isles.

In the Spring of 1541, James' second legitimate son, Robert, was born, but both he and his older brother died on 21st April of that year. Both King and Queen were distraught. The children were buried at Holyrood, next to Queen Madeleine.

During 1541, James seriously considered visiting England, to hold a conference with his uncle, Henry VIII at York. It appears that the English thought this was a definite arrangement, whilst James did not believe he had actually committed himself to it. James' failure to appear at York was held against him by Henry, who believed he had been humiliated by his nephew. Later that year, James attended the funeral of his mother at Perth.

The uneasy peace that had obtained between Scotland and England since the late 1520s (border raids by local reivers excepted) began to break down. By and large, border raids were ignored as casus belli unless they took place under the direct orders of either King or were led by his lieutenants. In early 1541, the English Duke of Norfolk led a massive raid into the south-east of Scotland, but was defeated by Scots, under the leadership of George Gordon, 4th Earl of Huntly, at Haddon Rig (14).

What was intended as a retaliatory raid, in the west went horribly wrong when James' troops were scattered or imprisoned at Solway Moss (15) on 24th November 1542. Within three weeks of the battle, James had died at Falkland Palace. He was interred next to Queen Madeleine and his sons at Holyrood.

Key to Map

1. Linlithgow Castle

2. Stirling Castle

3. Edinburgh Castle

4. Craigmillar Castle

5. Falkland Palace

6. Holyrood Palace

7. Tantallon Castle

8. Balcomie Castle, Fife

9. Inverary

10. Blair Atholl Castle

11. Crawford Castle

12. Jedburgh

13. Aberdeen

14. Haddon Rigg

15. Solway Moss

Chapter 11: Book Review

There is a dearth of modern, easily available books on James V. Most works touching on him are broader histories, or dense academic works concentrating on a particular theme. The most accessible information is in Linda Porter's *'Crown of Thistles'*

Crown of Thistles: The fatal inheritance of Mary, Queen of Scots

Author: Dr Linda Porter

Publisher: Macmillan

In a nutshell: An original take on a tale that has been told many times. Excellent both for readers new to the period and experts.

The sub-title of this book refers to the fatal inheritance of Mary, Queen of Scots, but this is actually a panoramic look at the relationship between the monarchs of England and Scotland between the 1480s and the Union of the Crowns in 1603 – although the period of Mary's incarceration in England and the 15 years after her death are dealt with more as a tidying up of loose ends.

Porter manages to convey a huge amount of information about all of the protagonists in very readable format. The depth of her research across the whole spectrum of people and events is impressive.

This extensive knowledge has allowed Porter to contest some of the frequently repeated judgements on many of the people and events involved. For example she is kinder to Margaret Tudor, the widow of James IV than most historians have been – seeing Margaret as well-intentioned and determined to do the best for her son's realm. She also challenges the frequently repeated assertion that, post-Flodden, with a generation of leaders dead on the field, Scotland descended into chaos.

This is not, however, a dreary recitation of political facts. Porter covers a wide range of topics, from the architectural interests of Henry VIII, and the literary pursuits of James V, to the religious views of John Knox and the Machiavellian plotting of Mary's mother-in-law, Catherine de Medici.

Porter's Mary, too, is more nuanced than is often the case. She is shown as physically extremely courageous, charismatic, resourceful and politically shrewd in many ways, but Porter hints, although does not conclude, that Mary was probably aware of the plot to murder Darnley, even if she were not directly responsible.

Mary's actions after the death of Darnley seem to fly in the face of common sense, but hindsight is a marvellous thing, and it is difficult to unknow the results. At the time, Mary was surrounded by factions and traitors and each individual choice she made can be justified, although the outcome was disastrous. Her worst mistake of all was stepping into the fishing boat that took her across the Solway Firth and into twenty years of incarceration at the hands of her cousin, Elizabeth I.

The book is a weighty tome, but I wish it had been longer. An exposition by Porter of the years of plot and counterplot as Mary was pitted against Elizabeth's spymaster, Sir Francis Walsingham would make gripping reading.

Bibliography

Accounts of the Treasurer of Scotland: v. 5-8:. Edinburgh: H.M. General Register House, 1877

Calendar of State Papers: Domestic Series: Edward VI, 1547-1553. United Kingdom: Stationery Office Books.

Calendar of State Papers Simancas, British History Online (HMSO, 1892) Hume, Martin A S, ed.,

Calendar of State Papers: Venice <http://www.british-history.ac.uk/cal-state-papers/venice/vol2/vii-lxi> [accessed 7 October 2015]

Charters and Documents Relating to the City of Glasgow 1175 - 1649, British History Online <http://www.british-history.ac.uk/glasgow-charters/1175-1649/no2/pp79-87> [accessed 17 September 2015]

Letters and Papers, Foreign and Domestic, of the Reign of Henry VIII: Preserved in the Public Record Office, the British Museum, and Elsewhere in England (United Kingdom: British History Online, 2014) https://www.british-history.ac.uk/letters-papers-hen8/ Brewer, John Sherren, and James Gairdner

http://www.nas.gov.uk/downloads/jamesIIIDeath.pdf   [accessed   17 September 2015]

Records of the Parliaments of Scotland <http://www.rps.ac.uk/> [accessed 17 September 2015]

Sadler, Sir Ralph, *The State Papers and Letters of Sir Ralph Sadler in 3 Volumes*, ed. by Arthur Clifford (Edinburgh: Archibald Constable & Co., 1809)

Thesaurariorum Regum Scotorum (Edinburgh: H.M. General Register House, 1877)

Coltman, Dayle, and Gordon Donaldso:, *The Edinburgh History of Scotland: James V-James VII v. 3* (The Edinburgh History of Scotland) (Edinburgh: Hyperion Books, 1998)

De Nicolay, Nicolas: *The Navigation of James V Round Scotland, the Orkney Isles and the Hebrides or Western Isles*

De Lisle, Leanda, *Tudor: The Family Story* (United Kingdom: Chatto & Windus, 2013)

Drummond, William, ed., *The History of Scotland from the Year 1423 until the Year 1542, Containing the Lives and Reigns of James I, II, III, IV and V* (London: H Hills for R Tomlins and himself, 1655)

Eaves, Richard Glen: *Henry VIII and James V's Regency, 1524-1528: A Study in Anglo-Scottish Diplomacy* (Lanham: University Press of America, 1987)

Ellis, Henry, *Original Letters, Illustrative of English History: Including Numerous Royal Letters: From Autographs in the British Museum, the State Paper Office, and One or Two Other Collections.*, 1st edn (New York: Printed for Harding, Triphook, & Lepard, 1824)

Fraser, Antonia, *Mary Queen of Scots* (London: HarperCollins Publishers, 1970)

Gibb, George Duncan: *The Life and Times of Robert Gib. Lord of Caribber, Famililar Servitor and Master of the Stable to King James V of Scotland* (London: Longmans, Green & Co., 1874)

Guy, J. (2004) *My Heart is My Own: the Life of Mary Queen of Scots.* London: Harper Perennial.

Hall, Edward, *Hall's Chronicle.* (S.l.: Ams Press, 1909)

Holinshed, Raphael, *Holinshed's Chronicles of England, Scotland & Ireland* (United Kingdom: AMS Press, 1997)

Hotle, Patrick C.: *Thorns and Thistles: Diplomacy between Henry VIII and James V, 1528-1542* (Lanham, MD: University Press of America, 1996)

Keith, Robert: *History of the Affairs of Church and State in Scotland from the Beginning of the Reformation to the Year 1568* (Edinburgh: Spottiswoode, 1844),

Lang, Andrew, *The History of Scotland from the Roman Occupation: Vol III C. 79 - 1545*, 3rd edn (New York: Dodd, Mead & Co., 1903)

Lemon, Robert, ed., *Calendar of State Papers: Domestic Series: Edward, Mary and Elizabeth*, British History Online (London: HMSO, 1856)

Lindsay of Pitscottie, Robert, *Pitscottie's Chronicles of Scotland*, ed. by Ae. J. G Mackay (Edinburgh: Blackwood for the Society, 1911)

Marshall, R. K. (2003) *Scottish Queens 1034 - 1714*. United Kingdom: Tuckwell Press.

Marshall, Rosalind Kay, *Queen Mary's Women: Female Relatives, Servants, Friends and Enemies of Mary, Queen of Scots* (Edinburgh: John Donald Publishers, 2006)

Oliver, Neil: *A History of Scotland* (Phoenix PR, 2011)

Perry, Maria: *Sisters to the King*, 2nd edn (Andre Deutsch, 2002)

Pitcairn, Robert: *Criminal Trials in Scotland from AD 1488 to AD 1624* (Edinburgh: William Tait, 1833)

Porter, Linda, *Crown of Thistles: The Fatal Inheritance of Mary Queen of Scots* (United Kingdom: Macmillan, 2013)

Reese, Peter, *Flodden: A Scottish Tragedy (Birlinn)* (Edinburgh: Birlinn Publishers, 2003)

Reid, Stuart, *Battles of the Scottish Lowlands* (Barnsley: Pen & Sword Military, 2004)

Ritchie, P. E. (2002) *Mary of Guise in Scotland, 1548-1560: A Political Study*. United Kingdom: Tuckwell Press.

Starkey, David, *The Reign of Henry VIII: Personalities and Politics* (Vintage 3 October 2002)

Stedall, Robert, *The Challenge to the Crown: The Struggle for Influence in the Reign of Mary, Queen of Scots 1542 - 1567,* 1st edn (Sussex, England: Book Guild Publishing, 2012)

Strickland, Agnes, Lives Of The Queens Of Scotland And English Princesses V2: Connected With The Regal Succession Of Great Britain (Harper & Brothers, 1859), i & ii

Thomson, John Maitland, ed., *The Register of the Great Seal of Scotland* (Edinburgh: HM General Register House, 1894)

Thornton, T. (2009) *Henry VIII's Progress Through Yorkshire in 1541 and its Implications for Northern Identities, Northern History,* 46(2), pp. 231–244. doi: 10.1179/174587009x452323.

www.tudortimes.co.uk

Printed in Great Britain
by Amazon